Till Tales
Seeds for new dawns

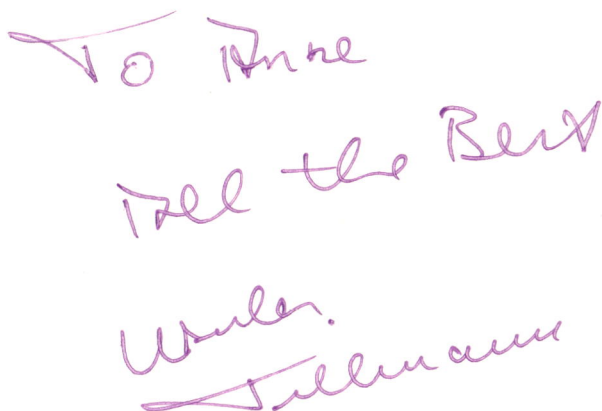

by
Ursula Tillmann

Till Tales
Seeds for new dawns

Copyright © 2007 by Ursula Tillmann
Cover–Photo by Ursula Tillmann
Location: Pebble Beach, CA, Inn at Spanish Bay – 2007

All rights reserved under International and Pan-American copyright conventions. No part of this book may be reproduced, stored in a retrieval system or transmitted in any form, electronic, mechanical, or by other means, without written permission of the author.

Library of Congress
Cataloging in Publication Data

ISBN 0-7951-8805-6

Manufactured in The United States of America by
Watermark Press
3600 Crondall Lane
Suite 100
Owings Mills, MD 21117

I dedicate my first publication to my parents, Waltraud and Gunther Tillmann. With thanks, for giving me the backbone to never lose sight and stay on my path.

Ursula Tillmann

Content-Sections:

Travels 7

Silence Within 17

Beyond Shadows 25

Breaking waves 33

Letters 43

Momentos 49

Search and Wait 55

Travels

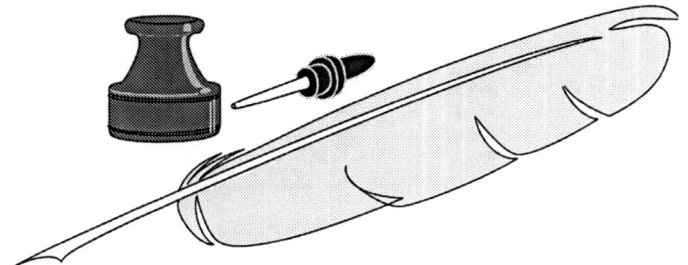

Till Tales   Seeds for new dawn

Gone to Gemaris

Free fall and dive
into new dawns.
Endless space, horizons
lost on causes
left for others
to bigger about.

Gone to Gemaris
way beyond chocolate
covered milky ways
diluting the purpose.
Escaped by choice to
my private space.

In time, settled by
dreams cried out loud
with stories told to
hold my fantasies
of wizards and awes
the way, I can see them.

Ursula Tillmann

Travels

And even though
I had wandered
a thousand miles
toward my destination,

I realized, when reaching
the place, I had longed
for all those years, that
only shadows were there –

Way back, hundreds
of miles, of days –
which I had experienced
with always different sunrises –

I had passed my destination.
Way back – too late now,
the roads backward
in time are closed ...

Planted dreams

Wilted the blossom
of planted dreams
out there, on my
field of memories.

Time could not
force itself to
deposit
duration.

Pining away
with that
last breath
toward the bud.

Ursula Tillmann

The stranger

Your face resembles
a memory – past due
without a name attached.

Wondering, why we can talk
with so much ease about your
deepest frights and joys.

When you curl your lips
to grasp the content of
my journey through time,

You remind me of another,
once familiar on my path,
ready to finally listen.

Our good-bye will be painless
when we depart – as we met,
without attachment ...

Regards to ...

Cold winds
emerging
my fears
of being
held ...

Gentle
warmth
somewhere
beneath...

But – no exit
this side
of broadway ...

Ursula Tillmann

New lands

The sound of spring
awakens me to new life –
New thoughts, which
I believed forgotten
in long winter nights.

The air so mild, the
smell of green grass,
the sound of splashing
creeks and rivers – calling
me out of my isolation.

Somewhere I hear birds
twitter – passing by
on their way up north.
And I long to travel with
them – to new lands ...

Till Tales   Seeds for new dawn

The wind

I can feel the wind today
stronger than ever
whipping away my tears
of solitude and loneliness.

No longer do I feel him
overpowering me –
we are one – in need
of each other ...

Arrival

Finally there,
and within –
all of me and
more to come.

Shedding off
dust from
detours, not
anticipated.

Tilling my
own gardens
finally for
my harvest.

Silence within

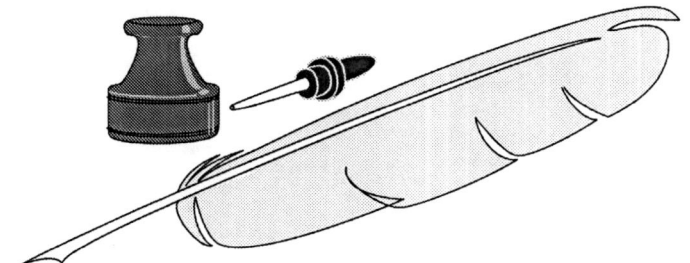

Silence within

Silence within, quiet from
sorrow and pain taken away
by the striking clock of spells.

Side by side resting at last,
unwilling close together. No more
dawns to frighten new horizons.

Painful words gusted by
the evening breeze, dissolving
the formation of new storms.

Gone are the shadows, which
clouded your vision of
possibilities left untouched.

Battlegrounds have lost their
trenches, competing for my affection
when I left, before you turned away.

Silence within, quiet now, too soon.
A single tear cannot water all
those roses, I planted on your graves ...

Ursula Tillmann

Night

Sleep will not
rest upon
my dreams –
The candle burns
before its time.
Lost causes
chase the
striking clock
and moments
weep their memories.

Before this day
will dawn again
I seek rebirth
with all its pain –
longing for comfort
of that child –
which slept
and dreamt
and rested
at night ...

Homeless

Her face sunburnt and stained
from soil, she calls her home
for just a blink of her existence,
carrying like make-up –
the burden of city-glitter,
covering the cause of reasons.

Heavy weighs the load of
collections, which make up a
life-time, bundled up in one
black garbage-bag, dragged
behind her footsteps on newly
paved sidewalks for other uses.

Her bulky coat, sweeping the way
busy pedestrians try to avoid,
to catch the eye, that views the
march – as useless as hers.
A cigarette, sometimes a dime,
her daily bread will be provided.

But under shady trees, familiar
faces, with lesser loads to
carry on, recognizing with
a smile, perhaps even her name.
With hope now, marching on she will,
while city lights are dimmed ...

Ursula Tillmann

Sleepers

Endless white
and still, so still ...
The sleepers are
dreaming beneath
a crust of
frozen crystals.

No warmth to
hold and melt
their efforts.

Still, so still
and endless white.
Waiting for warmer
days to uncover,
what lies beneath ...

Last Exit

Yellow paint on barren walls
covering the obvious, behind
wooden doors without knobs.

Forbidden hallways for residents
with no extension on their lease.
Lit exit signs marking the path.

The smell of decay mixed
with freshly brewed coffee
watering down the effect.

Searching, with eyes so dull,
a glimpse of withering spirit,
reaching for a straw to bail out.

Sighting her for one last smile,
a spark, her fragile body
still neatly groomed.

"Enough," I think, "all then in vain?"
Her tired hand now softly reaching
and petting, what's left of me.

Beyond Shadows

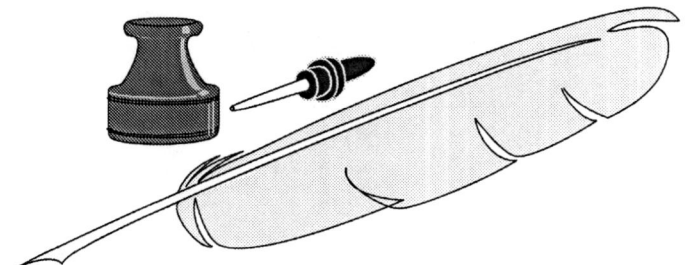

For You

I am resting my
thoughts to higher
plains, to ridges
no man has ever
climbed or ridden.
Beyond shadows, where
agony once stood
guard at my gate.

My keepers
have surrendered
their efforts
to hold down
my attempts
to face another day,
not daring to
look into my face.

They too know
of places I could
hide to regain strength.
Pacing my options
within three yards of
sanity, I am resting
my thought for
you, my love.

Ursula Tillmann

Hope

Rugged mountains
cannot hinder
the view beyond
caged thoughts –
treasured for
too many moons.

Beyond the range
there is a vision
grassing my mind.
Hope nourished
by friends
touching gently.

The chilly breeze
will not melt
beneath my skin.
I know the warmth
of new dreams
beyond tomorrow ...

GONE

Lay me softly,
hold me still.

Let the candle
burn all night –
and the breeze
cooling my
pasture of hopes.

Lay me softly,
when I go.

Hold me still,
when I am done ...

Ursula Tillmann

Moment of Victory

You are sneaking
under my starched
blanket of thoughts
to reason the
stories you told
yourself for others.

My skin is wearing
my emotions
too tight to
crack down at the
dawn of morning
to let go ...

You are soaking
the moment of victory
for your age to come.
Me and myself are
left beyond doubts
of self defence.

Linger

Linger a while and
help me hold my breath
while synchronizing
my scrambled thoughts.

Do not shut the
windows yet –
the night will soon
enough break the day ...

Ursula Tillmann

Dreamers

Stillness around,
the night has
closed to find
its dreamers.
We are dreamers
of broken
illusions.

We dream
the dream
and hope
the thought
what might,
and should,
but isn't ...

We care
to dare
what could,
but will not.
We are dreamers,
and the night
won't last ...

Breaking waves

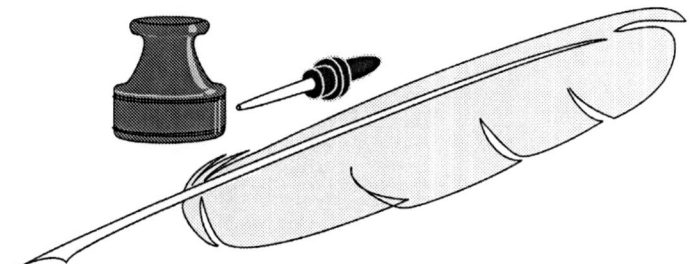

I am

I am the
gentle breeze,
soothing
your mind
like velvet,
covering with
my blanket
your grief
of yesterdays
thoughts ...

I am the
wild ocean,
breaking
its waves
on your shores
of my memories,
soaking with
salty waters
the current
to pause ...

Ursula Tillmann

To the sea ...

Gently touching
sandy beaches,
withdrawing tenderly.
Holding hands within.
The current of
stillness beyond.

Birds gliding, breaking
the alto of waves,
becoming one in
harmony, dissolving
and diving into
new concertos ...

Till Tales   Seeds for new dawn

Standing tall

My tears
have dried
my memories ...

Standing alone
at the shore,
waiting for the current

To break new
lands beneath
my feet ...

But drifting,
vanishing
too soon ...

To stand tall
for all those
moments to come ...

Ursula Tillmann

Brave ...

Brave and
strong like
the current
of the ocean
with its endless
power dancing
to the drum
of nature,
coming and
letting go,
day after day –
endless,
restless,
useless ...

Forgotten

Forgotten dreams
of lost horizons
beyond those ocean waves
breaking, knocking,
demanding all ...

Floating with sounds
the wind has echoed –
between waves, before
they reach the shore
to claim their prize ...

Ursula Tillmann

Now

Embracing
the vanishing
moment ...

Like quick-sand
reaching out,
trying to hold ...

Gone to shore
and new
encounters ...

Soaking in
one last glimpse
of my dream ...

Endless

Endless my
vision – without
shores – like the
ocean out there.

Nothing to
hold back
nor to tie down
endless moments.

Dissolving,
becoming one
with all and
yet nothing.

Letters

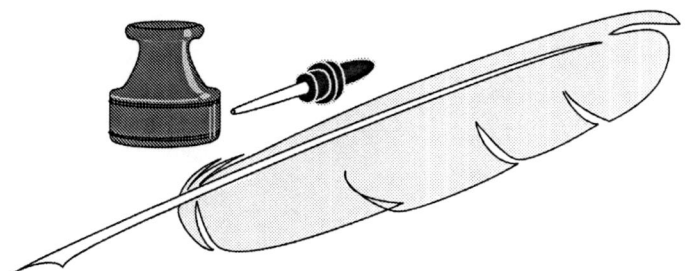

Distant land

Dear Wilhelm,

You are in such a distant land
for so many month now, that I had
to look at your photograph
again on the fireplace mantle,
to remember the shape of your lips,
curling up to that grin on your face.

I hope, you are still wearing that black
leather pilot-cap with the white scarf,
I made for you last winter. Remember?
You know, the one that's pictured in
the portrait you gave to me,
before you said good-bye.

Your sister is keeping herself so busy,
she doesn't say, but we know, it's
her way of burying her fear.
I did not show her those last lines,
you wrote to me from the front, I could
feel the pain through the ink of your pen.

When the officer phoned me this morning,
I hesitated to pick up the receiver.
I knew already, he did not have to say.
Tonight he will bring the rest of you belongings.
Where are you now? I am writing this
letter for keeps, for your children ...

Ursula Tillmann

Deep South

Dear Magda,

When I close my eyes, I can still smell the
mixture of sweet perfume and foul water,
the sweat of my skin scenting the
stillness of the air in Louisiana.
The humidity choking new beginnings
after that tragic day last September.

You should have celebrated your
birthday, as you promised your friends.
But I knew then, that time had no
opportunity to keep pace with your desires.
I hope, you found him and are resting
your agonies without further delay.

That letter you left, is still
in the box, you packed so neatly
the night before. Why couldn't
you have waited for winter, for
shorter days to end such young illusions?
I still believe you could have made it.

But, two years wasn't enough
time to cope after his departure.
Did you hear his voice, quietly
calling in the stillness of the night?
Did he demand, that you should
follow once again for his sake?

Till Tales   Seeds for new dawn

Departure

Dear Lover,

I have stepped out
of your circle of
circumstances, that
would not promise
duration for my
ways to come.

I have left on
the lights in the
hallway, so you
would find your
way back to your
accustomed path.

Farewell my love
I am leaving this note,
while packing my destiny
into my own suitcase,
with less weight than
allowed for departures ...

Ursula Tillmann

Your shadows

Dear friend,

Your fear is so real to me,
that I can almost touch your
shadows, as if they were mine.
Do not explain, I can read
your eyes way beyond the
pupil of your expressions.

I have dived down there to
see the darkness, you can't share.
There is no bottom to this ocean.
I would have liked to replenish the
waters, calmed those rough waves
and anchored your destination.

But how do I tell a fish to swim
toward a new horizon, when it is
captured in that small aquarium,
circling six inches in one breath
and length toward the
shadows in front and beyond?

Momentos

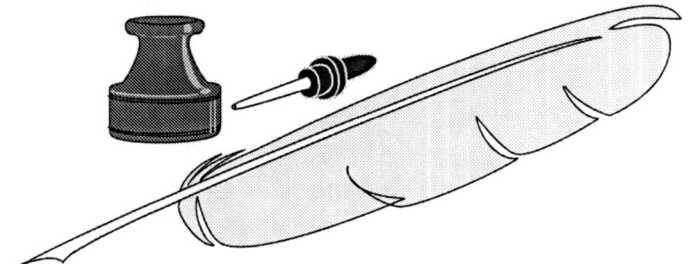

Till Tales   Seeds for new dawn

Do not step closer
toward me, than
I am to myself.

*

You have mowed
the lawns on my
field of efforts,
but then forgot
to set the sprinklers
for hope of new growth.

*

Where does the music go,
when the conductor has
silenced those violins,
playing Mahlers 5th adagio.
Stillness now, the crowd
has left for appetizers,
hungry for more ...

*

Instant gratification
on demand now
not later or forever.
Instant – in time
forgotten, but dished
out now on plastic plates ...

(continued)

Ursula Tillmann

*

With which form of silence
will you point toward solutions,
when our closeness requires
distance again ...

*

Someday soon, you
will grab my shoulders,
and shake my world:
"Wake up, it was
nothing but a dream.
Reality is for sleepers."

*

I can feel your closeness,
although you are not here.
I can read your thoughts,
although we are not talking.
Our distance is only in time –
we will overcome someday soon.

*

We should search
for something joyful –
instead for ourselves...

(continued)

Till Tales   *Seeds for new dawn*

During my last attempt
to shop, I left the basket
with my illusions at the till.
I could not bear the shoving
at the cashiers end to check
out with the burden of
promises on sale ...

*

Night-time knows no
boundaries when we fall.
It leans back and gazes
with astonishment at
the depth of its purpose.

*

What time?
Which day?
And where,
if at all?
Be quiet, all
has been said.

Search and Wait

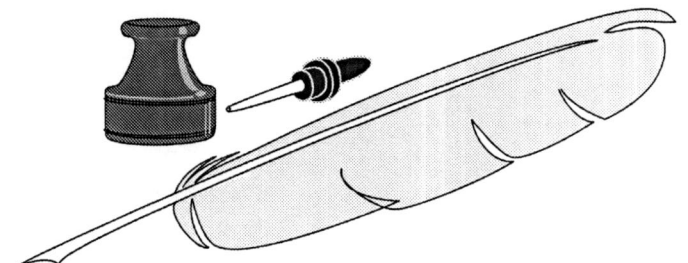

The wait

For hours, she had been looking out of the window with expectations. But, he wouldn't come today. She knew. And yet – she did not want to know. So she kept on waiting.

Even the shadow of a stray dog crossing the street, lifted her hopes – he still night come. After all, something moved on the street, something was happening. So why not his appearance? It would fit into her thinking.

"Aren't you coming for supper," she heard a voice from downstairs, "you haven't been with us since breakfast." She ignored the question. Why listen, when you are occupied with waiting. And waiting took all her efforts, exhausting her without needing any further strains.

Maybe the bus, she thought, or maybe a car? She should not neglect to pay attention to those vehicles. They carry people, don't they? And then again – he'd never come by bus. Oh no, she knew better. He'd be walking down that road, his trench-coat would move in a certain way, swinging with his light steps. She would sense him, miles away by instinct.

Didn't she always listen to that voice insider herself? Why was it so quiet today? Why didn't she feel him coming down that lane, he was long overdue.

"What's with your supper, should I keep it warm?" Again that interruption from downstairs.

She felt dizzy, somewhat weary. Her eyes began burning. "But I mustn't stop now hoping," she told herself. And again, she watched that lane, that road, which should bring him back. Thinking back, way back, tears filled her eyes. The sky began looking foggy. She wished them away. No tears now, she whispered. She could miss seeing him coming toward the house.

Her back felt tired, but she did not dare to give herself a rest, "If I lay down now, he will come," she convinced herself. I must remain alert and wait, or I will miss him."

It was her seventh week. "How long did you say, she has been standing at that window," the doctor asked her niece, while checking her blood pressure.

"No," she tried to whisper, "I mustn't fall asleep now, he'll come. I know too well, because I have waited so long ..."

She could hardly be heard, uttering those words, trying to lift her head. The doctor pushed her gently back into the cushions.

Hours passed. Or was it days?

"He is coming, I can see him, he is waving. I knew, he would come," she whispered, while trying to lift her head. "I am so glad you haven't forgotten, I knew, you would come, my dear Antoine. I have known it all along, I could feel it, hoping, that you knew it too ..."

"What did she say," the doctor asked. "Antoine? Did he not pass away two years ago."

The Search

"Have you seen him?" My question may as well have been the answer, when I looked into her eyes, knowing.

"No lately," a shallow voice whispered.

"Lately as in today or last week", my inquisition continued.

"Maybe, and maybe not. Who keeps track of time. Yes, I did see him, but not recently."

I should have anticipated, that this was not going anywhere, without further pressure in voice and posture.

"Why then and where, if at all. And right now," I demanded.

My inquiry was now met with silence. And my search seemed at a still stand. Eyes sparkling with anger, lips curling, ready to close down whispers of truth and possessiveness from either side. I could feel the dampness of the early evening creeping up my spine. Time was important, he may be searching too, I was hoping.

"When will you know, if lately was recently or just a short while ago," I continued.

Maybe I should have trusted my intuition, which mostly tells the answer, prior to the question. But then – who wouldn't prefer a detailed explanation, just to watch the struggle for excuses spinning into even bigger lies.

"Who cares what time, the why and when," I heard her saying now. "Isn't it always the same story, doesn't your search tell you all there needs to be known. Don't you understand absence as a means of ones own comfort and expression?'

I looked at her in amazement now, keeping silent.

She too. Why was I surprised?.

I think, I started to like her then, when I saw her eyes filling with tears, as she turned away quickly to walk toward the park.

Printed in the United States
200450BV00002B/19-288/A